The Expulsive Power of a New Affection

The Expulsive Power of a New Affection

Annotated

Thomas Chalmers

Cedar Lake Classics

Copyright © 2024 by Cedar Lake Classics

This is a proofread and newly designed edition of a public domain work.

CONTENTS

1 The Expulsive Power of a New Affection   1

ABOUT THIS BOOK   25
LIFE OF THOMAS CHALMERS   29

1

The Expulsive Power of a New Affection

"Love not the world, neither the things that are in the world. If any man love the world, the love of the Father is not in him." 1 John ii. 15.

THERE are two ways in which a practical moralist may attempt to displace from the human heart its love of the world - either by a demonstration of the world's vanity, so as that the heart shall be prevailed upon simply to withdraw its regards from an object that is not worthy of it; or, by setting forth another object, even God, as more worthy of its attachment, so as that the heart shall be prevailed upon not to resign an old affection, which shall have nothing to succeed it, but to exchange an old affection for a new one.

My purpose is to show, that from the constitution of our nature, the former method is altogether incompetent and ineffectual and that the latter method will alone suffice for the rescue and recovery of the heart from the wrong affection that domineers over it. After having accomplished this purpose, I shall attempt a few practical observations.

Love may be regarded in two different conditions.

1. **The first** is, when its object is at a distance, and then it becomes love in a state of desire.

2. **The second** is, when its object is in possession, and then it becomes love in a state of indulgence.

Under the impulse of desire, man feels himself urged onward in some path or pursuit of activity for its gratification. The faculties of his mind are put into busy exercise. In the steady direction of one great and engrossing interest, his attention is recalled from the many reveries into which it might otherwise have wandered; and the powers of his body are forced away from an indolence in which it else might have languished; and that time is crowded with occupation, which but for some object of keen and devoted ambition, might have drivelled along in successive hours of weariness and distaste - and though hope does not always enliven, and success does not always crown this career of exertion, yet in the midst of this very variety, and with the alternations of occasional disappointment, is the machinery of the whole man kept in a sort of congenial play, and upholden in that tone and temper which are most agreeable to it.

Insomuch, that if, through the extirpation of that desire which forms the originating principle of all this movement,

THE EXPULSIVE POWER OF A NEW AFFECTION

the machinery were to stop, and to receive no impulse from another desire substituted in its place, the man would be left with all his propensities to action in a state of most painful and unnatural abandonment. A sensitive being suffers, and is in violence, if, after having thoroughly rested from his fatigue, or been relieved from his pain, he continue in possession of powers without any excitement to these powers; if he possess a capacity of desire without having an object of desire; or if he have a spare energy upon his person, without a counterpart, and without a stimulus to call it into operation.

The misery of such a condition is often realized by him who is retired from business, or who is retired from law, or who is even retired from the occupations of the chase, and of the gaming table. Such is the demand of our nature for an object in pursuit, that no accumulation of previous success can extinguish it - and thus it is, that the most prosperous merchant, and the most victorious general, and the most fortunate gamester, when the labour of their respective vocations has come to a close, are often found to languish in the midst of all their acquisitions, as if out of their kindred and rejoicing element. It is quite in vain with such a constitutional appetite for employment in man, to attempt cutting away from him the spring or the principle of one employment, without providing him with another. Thu whole heart and habit will rise in resistance against such an undertaking. The else unoccupied female who spends the hours of every evening at some play of hazard, knows as well as you, that the pecuniary gain, or the honourable triumph of a successful contest, are altogether paltry. It is not such a demonstration of vanity as this that will force her away from her dear and delightful occupatiou. The habit cannot so be displaced, as to leave nothing but a negative and cheerless vacancy behind it - though it may so be supplanted as to be followed up by another habit of employment, to which the power of some new affection has constrained her. It is willingly suspended, for example, on any single evening, should the time that wont to be allotted to gaining, require to be spent on the preparations of an approaching assembly. The ascendant power of a second affection will do, what no exposition however forcible, of the folly and worthlessness of the first, ever could effectuate.

And it is the same in the great world. We shall never be able to arrest any of its leading pursuits, by a naked demonstration of their vanity. It is quite in vain to think of stopping one of these pursuits in any way else, but by stimulating to another. In attempting to bring a worldly man intent and busied with the prosecution of his objects to a dead stand, we have not merely to encounter the charm which he annexes to these objects - but we have to encounter the pleasure which he feels in the very prosecution of them. It is not enough, then, that we dissipate the charm, by a moral, and eloquent, and affecting exposure of its illusiveness. We must address to the eye of his mind another object, with a charm powerful enough to dispossess the first of its influences, and to engage him in some other prosecution as full of interest, and hope, and congenial activity, as the former.

It is this which stamps an impotency on all moral and pathetic declamation about the insignificance of the world. A man will no more consent to the misery of being without an

THE EXPULSIVE POWER OF A NEW AFFECTION

object, because that object is a trifle, or of being without a pursuit, because that pursuit terminates in some frivolous or fugitive acquirement, than he will voluntarily submit himself to the torture, because that torture is to be of short duration. If to be without desire and without exertion altogether, is a state of violence and discomfort, then the present desire, with its correspondent train of exertion, is not to be got rid of simply by destroying it. It must be by substituting another desire, and another line or habit of exertion in its place - and the most effectual way of withdrawing the mind from one object, is not by turning it away upon desolate and unpeopled vacancy - but by presenting to its regards another object still more alluring.

These remarks apply not merely to love considered in its state of desire for an object not yet obtained. They apply also to love considered in its state of indulgence, or placid gratification, with an object already in possession. It is seldom that any of our tastes are made to disappear by a mere process of natural extinction. At least, it is very seldom, that this is done through the instrumentality of reasoning. It may be done by excessive pampering - but it is almost never done by the mere force of mental determination. But what cannot be destroyed, may be dispossessed and one taste may be made to give way to another, and to lose its, power entirely as the reigning affection of the mind.

It is thus, that the boy ceases, at length, to be the slave of his appetite, but it is because a manlier taste has now brought it into subordination - and that the youth ceases to idolize pleasure, but it is because the idol of wealth has become the stronger and gotten the aseendancy and that even the love of money ceases to have the mastery over the heart of many a thriving citizen, but it is because drawn into, the whirl of city polities, another affection has been wrought into his moral system, and he is now lorded over by the love of power. There is not one of these transformations in which the heart is left without an object. Its desire for one particular object may be conquered; but as to its desire for having some one object or other, this is unconquerable. Its adhesion to that on which it has fastened the preference of its regards, cannot willingly be overcome by the rending away of a simple separation. It can be done only by the application of something else, to which it may feel the adhesion of a still stronger and more powerful preference. Such is the grasping tendency of the human heart, that it must have something to lay hold of - and which, if wrested away without the substitution of another something in its place, would leave a void and a vacancy as painful to the mind, as hunger is to the natural system. It may be dispossessed of one object, or of any, but it cannot be desolated of all. Let there be a breathing and a sensitive heart, but without a liking and without affinity to any of the things that are around it; and, in a state of cheerless abandonment, it would be alive to nothing but the burden of its own consciousness, and feel it to be intolerable. It would make no difference to its owner, whether he dwelt in the midst of a gay and goodly world; or, placed afar beyond the outskirts of creation, he dwelt a solitary unit in dark and unpeopled nothingness. The heart must have something to cling to - and never, by its own voluntary consent, will it so denude itself of its attachments, that there shall not be one remaining object that can draw or solicit it.

The misery of a heart thus bereft of all relish for that which wont to minister enjoyment, is strikingly exemplified in those, who, satiated with indulgence, have been so belaboured, as it were, with the variety and the poignancy of the pleasurable sensations they have experienced, that they are at length fatigued out of all capacity for sensation whatever. The disease of ennui is more frequent in the French metropolis, where amusement is more exclusively the occupation of the higher classes, than it is in the British metropolis, where the longings of the heart are more diversified by the resources of business and politics.

There are the votaries of fashion who, in this way, have at length become the victims of fashionable excess - in whom the very multitude of their enjoyments, has at last extinguished their power of enjoyment - who, with the gratifications of art and nature at command, now look upon all that is around them with an eye of tastelessness - who, plied with the delights of sense and of splendour even to weariness, and incapable of higher delights, have come to the end of all their perfection, and like Solomon of old, found it to be vanity and vexation. The man whose heart has thus been turned into a desert, can vouch for the insupportable languor which must ensue, when one affection is thus plucked away from the bosom, without another to replace it. It is not necessary that a man receive pain from anything, in order to become miserable. It is barely enough that he looks with distaste to everything - and in that asylum which is the repository of minds out of joint, and where the organ of feeling as well as the organ of intellect, has been impaired, it is not in the cell of loud and frantic outcries, where we shall meet with the acme of mental suffering. But that is the individual who outpeers in wretchedness all his fellows, who, throughout the whole expanse of nature and society, meets not an object that has at all the power to detain or to interest him; who, neither in earth beneath nor in heaven above, knows of a single charm to which his heart can send forth one desirous or responding movement; to whom the world, in his eye a vast and empty desolation, has left him nothing but his own consciousness to feed upon dead to all that is without him, and alive to nothing but to the load of his own torpid and useless existence.

It will now be seen, perhaps, why it is that the heart keeps by its present affections with so much tenacity - when the attempt is, to do them away by a mere process of extirpation. It will not consent to be so desolated. The strong man, whose dwelling-place is there, may be compelled to give way to another occupier - but unless another stronger than he, has power to dispossess and to succeed him, he will keep his present lodgment unviolable. The heart would revolt against its own emptiness. It could not bear to be so left in a state of waste and cheerless insipidity. The moralist who tries such a process of dispossession as this upon the heart, is thwarted at every step by the recoil of its own mechanism. You have all heard that Nature abhors a vacuum. Such at least is the nature of the heart, that though the room which is in it may change one inmate for another, it cannot be left void without the pain of most intolerable suffering. It is not enough then to argue the folly of an existing affection. It is not enough, in the terms of a forcible or an affecting demonstration, to make good the evanescence of its object. It may not even be enough to associate the threats and the terrors of some coming vengeance, with the indulgence of it. The heart may still resist every application, by obedience to which, it would finally be conducted to a state so much at war with all its appetites as that of downright inanition. So to tear away an affection from the heart, as to leave it bare of all its regards and of all its preferences, were a hard and hopeless undertaking - and it would appear, as if the alone powerful engine of dispossession were to bring the mastery of another affection to bear upon it.

We know not a more sweeping interdict upon the affections of Nature, than that which is delivered by the Apostle in the verse before us. To bid a man into whom there has not yet entered the great and ascendant influence of the principle of regeneration, to bid him withdraw his love from all the things that are in the world, is to bid him give up all the affections that are in his heart. The world is the all of a natural man. He has not a taste nor a desire, that points not to a something placed within the confines of its visible horizon. He loves nothing above it, and he cares for nothing beyond it; and to bid him love not the world, is to pass a sentence of expulsion on all the inmates of his bosom. To estimate the magnitude and the difficulty of such a surrender, let us only think that it were just as arduous to prevail on him not to love wealth, which is but one of the things in the world, as to prevail on him to set wilful fire to his own property. This he might do with sore and painful reluctance, if he saw that the salvation of his life hung upon it. But this he would do willingly, if he saw that a new property of tenfold value was instantly to emerge from the wreck of the old one.

In this case there is something more than the mere displacement of an affection. There is the overbearing of one affection by another. But to desolate his heart of all love for the things of the world, without the substitution of any love in its place, were to him a process of as unnatural violence, as to destroy all the things that he has in the world, and give him nothing in their room. So that, if to love not the world be indispensable to one's Christianity, then the crucifixion of the old man is not too strong a term to mark that transition in his history, when all old things are done away and all things become new. We hope that by this time, you understand the impotency of a mere demonstration of this world's insignificance. Its sole practical effect, if it had any, would be. to leave the heart in a state which to even heart is insupportable, and that is a mere state of nakedness and negation. You may remember the fond and unbroken tenacity with which your heart has often recurred to pursuits, over the utter frivolity of which it sighed and wept but yesterday. The arithmetic of your short-lived days, may on Sabbath make the clearest impression upon your understanding - and from his fancied bed of death, may the preacher cause a voice to descend in rebuke and mockery on all the pursuits of earthliness - and as he pictures before you the fleeting generations of men, with the absorbing grave, whither all the joys and interests of the world hasten to their sure and speedy oblivion, may you, touched and solemnized by his argument, feel for a moment

THE EXPULSIVE POWER OF A NEW AFFECTION

as if on the eve of a practical and permanent emancipation from a scene of so much vanity.

But the morrow comes, and the business of the world, and the objects of the world, and the moving forces of the world come along with it - and the machinery of the heart, in virtue of which it must have something to grasp, or something to adhere to, brings it under a kind of moral necessity to be actuated just as before - and in utter repulsion to wards a state so unkindly as that of being frozen out both of delight and of desire, does it feel all the warmth and the urgency of its wonted solicitations - nor in the habit and history of the whole man, can we detect so much as one symptom of the new creature - so that the church, instead of being to him a school of obedience, has been a mere sauntering place for the luxury of a passing and theatrical emotion; and the preaching which is mighty to compel the attendance of multitudes, which is mighty to still and to solemnize the hearers into a kind of tragic sensibility, which is mighty in the play of variety and vigour that it can keep up around the imagination, is not mighty to the pulling down of strong holds.

The love of the world cannot be expunged by a mere demonstration of the world's worthlessness. But may it not be supplanted by the love of that which is more worthy than itself? The heart cannot be prevailed upon to part with the world, by a simple act of resignation. But may not the heart be prevailed upon to admit into its preference another, who shall subordinate the world, and bring it down from its wonted ascendancy? If the throne which is placed there must have an occupier, and the tyrant that now reigns has occupied it wrongfully, he may not leave a bosom which would rather detain him than be left in desolation. But may he not give way to the lawful sovereign, appearing with every charm that can secure His willing admittance, and taking unto himself His great power to subdue the moral nature of man, and to reign over it? In a word, if the way to disengage the heart from the positive love of one great and ascendant object, is to fasten it in positive love to another, then it is not by exposing the worthlessness of the former, but by addressing to the mental eye the worth and excellence of the latter, that all old things are to be done away and all things are to become new. To obliterate all our present affections by simply expunging them, and so as to leave the seat of them unoccupied, would be to destroy the old character, and to substitute no new character in its place. But when they take their departure upon the ingress of other visitors; when they resign their sway to the power and the predominance of new affections; when, abandoning the heart to solitude, they merely give place to a successor who turns it into as busy a residence of desire and interest and expectation as before - there is nothing in all this to thwart or to overbear any of the laws of our sentient nature - and we see how, in fullest accordance with the mechanism of the heart, a great moral revolution may be made to take place upon it.

This, we trust, will explain the operation of that charm which accompanies the effectual preaching of the gospel. The love of God and the love of the world, are two affections, not merely in a state of rivalship, but in a state of enmity - and that so irreconcilable, that they cannot dwell together in the same bosom. We have already affirmed how impossible it were for the heart, by any innate elasticity of its own, to cast the world away from it; and thus reduce itself to a wilderness. The heart is not so constituted; and the only way to dispossess it of an old affection, is by the expulsive power of a new one. Nothing can exceed the magnitude of the required change in a man's character - when bidden as he is in the New Testament, to love not the world; no, nor any of the things that are in the world for this so comprehends all that is dear to him in existence, as to be equivalent to a command of self-annihilation.

But the same revelation which dictates so mighty an obedience, places within our reach as mighty an instrument of obedience. It brings for admittance to the very door of our heart, an affection which once seated upon its throne, will either subordinate every previous inmate, or bid it away. Beside the world, it places before the eye of the mind Him who made the world and with this peculiarity, which is all its own - that in the Gospel do we so behold God, as that we may love God. It is there, and there only, where God stands revealed as an object of confidence to sinners and where our desire after Him is not chilled into apathy, by that barrier of human guilt which intercepts every approach that is not made to Him through the appointed Mediator. It is the bringing in of this better hope, whereby we draw nigh unto God - and to live without hope, is to live without God; and if the heart be without God, then world will then have all the ascendancy. It is God apprehended by the believer as God in Christ, who alone can dispost it from this ascendancy. It is when He stands dismantled of the terrors which belong to Him as an offended lawgiver and when we are enabled by faith, which is

His own gift, to see His glory in the face of Jesus Christ, and to hear His beseeching voice, as it protests good will to men, and entreats the return of all who will to a full pardon and a gracious acceptance_it is then, that a love paramount to the love of the world, and at length expulsive of it, first arises in the regenerated bosom. It is when released from the spirit of bondage with which love cannot dwell, and when admitted into the number of God's children through the faith that is in Christ Jesus, the spirit of adoption is poured upon us - it is then that the heart, brought under the mastery of one great and predominant affection, is delivered from the tyranny of its former desires, in the only way in which deliverance is possible. And that faith which is revealed to us from heaven, as indispensable to a sinner's justification in the sight of God, is also the instrument of the greatest of all moral and spiritual achievements on a nature dead to the influence, and beyond the reach of every other application.

Thus may we come to perceive what it is that makes the most effective kind of preaching. It is not enough to hold out to the world's eye the mirror of its own imperfections. It is not enough to come forth with a demonstration, however pathetic, of the evanescent character of all its enjoyments. It is not enough to travel the walk of experience along with you, and speak to your own conscience and your own recollection, of the deceitfulness of the heart, and the deceitfulness of all that the heart is set upon. There is many a bearer of the Gospel message, who has not shrewdness of natural discernment enough, and who has not power of characteristic description enough, and who has not the talent of moral delineation enough, to present you with a vivid and faithful sketch of the existing follies of society. But that very corruption which he has not the faculty of representing in its visible details, he may practically be the instrument of eradicating in its principle. Let him be but a faithful expounder of the gospel testimony unable as he may be to apply a descriptive hand to the character of the present world, let him but report with accuracy the matter which revelation has brought to him from a distant world - unskilled as he is in the work of so anatomizing the heart, as with the power of a novelist to create a graphical or impressive exhibition of the worthlessness of its many affections - let him only deal in those mysteries of peculiar doctrine, on which the best of novelists have thrown the wantonness of their derision. He may not be able, with the eye of shrewd and satirical observation, to expose to the ready recognition of his hearers, the desires of worldliness but with the tidings of the gospel in commission, he may wield the only engine that can extirpate them. He cannot do what some have done, when, as if by the hand of a magician, they have brought out to view, from the hidden recesses of our nature, the foibles and lurking appetites which belong to it.

But he has a truth in his possession, which into whatever heart it enters, will, like the rod of Aaron, swallow up them all - and unqualified as he may be, to describe the old man in all the nicer shading of his natural and constitutional varieties, with him is deposited that ascendant influence under which the leading tastes and tendencies of the old man are destroyed, and he becomes a new creature in Jesus Christ our Lord.

Let us not cease then to ply the only instrument of

powerful and positive operation, to do away from you the love of the world. Let us try every legitimate method of finding access to your hearts for the love of Him who is greater than the world. For this purpose, let us, if possible, clear away that shroud of unbelief which so hides and darkens the face of the Deity. Let us insist on His claims to your affection - and whether in the shape of gratitude, or in the shape of esteem, let us never cease to affirm, that in the whole of that wondrous economy, the purpose of which is to reclaim a sinful world unto Himself - he, the God of love, so sets Himself forth in characters of endearment, that nought but faith, and nought but understanding, are wanting, on your part, to call forth the love of your hearts back again.

And here let us advert to the incredulity of a worldly man; when he brings his own sound and secular experience to bear upon the high doctrines of Christianity - when he looks on regeneration as a thing impossible - when feeling as he does, the obstinacies of his own heart on the side of things present, and casting an intelligent eye, much exercised perhaps in the observation of human life, on the equal obstinacies of all who are around him, he pronounces this whole matter about the crucifixion of the old man, and the resurrection of a new man in his place, to be in downright opposition to all that is known and witnessed of the real nature of humanity. We think that we have seen such men, who, firmly trenched in their own vigorous and homebred sagacity, and shrewdly regardful of all that passes before them through the week, and upon the scenes of ordinary business, look on that transition of the heart by which it gradually dies unto time, and awakens in all the life of a new-felt and ever-growing desire towards God, as a mere Sabbath speculation; and who thus, with all their attention engrossed upon the concerns of earthliness, continue unmoved, to the end of their days, amongst the feelings, and the appetites, and the pursuits of earthliness. If the thought of death, and another state of being after it, comes across them at all, it is not with a change so radical as that of being born again, that they ever connect the idea of preparation. They have some vague conception of its being quite enough that they acquit themselves in some decent and tolerable way of their relative obligations; and that, upon the strength of some such social and domestic moralities as are often realized by him into whose heart the love of God has never entered, they will be transplanted in safety from this world, where God is the Being with whom it may almost be said that they have had nothing to do, to that world where God is the Being with whom they will have mainly and immediately to do throughout all eternity. They admit all that is said of the utter vanity of time, when taken up with as a resting place. But they resist every application made upon the heart of man, with the view of so shifting its tendencies, that it shall not henceforth find in the interests of time, all its rest and all its refreshment. They, in fact, regard such an attempt as an enterprise that is altogether aerial - and with a tone of secular wisdom, caught from the familiarities of every-day experience, do they see a visionary character in all that is said of setting our affections on the things that are above; and of walking by faith; and of keeping our hearts - in such a love of God as shall shut out from them the love of the world; and of having no confidence in the flesh; and of so renouncing earthly things as to have our conversation in heaven.

Now, it is altogether worthy of being remarked of those men who thus disrelish spiritual Christianity, and, in fact, deem it an impracticable acquirement, how much of a piece their incredulity about the demands of Christianity, and their incredulity about the doctrines of Christianity, are with one another. No wonder that they feel the work of the New Testament to be beyond their strength, so long as they hold the words of the New Testament to be beneath their attention. Neither they nor anyone else can dispossess the heart of an old affection, but by the expulsive power of a new one - and, if that new affection be the love of God, neither they nor anyone else can be made to entertain it, but on such a representation of the Deity, as shall draw the heart of the sinner towards Him. Now it is just their unbelief which screens from the discernment of their minds this representation. They do not see the love of God in sending His Son unto the world. They do not see the expression of His tenderness to men, in sparing Him not, but giving Him up unto the death for us all. They do not see the sufficiency of the atonement, or the sufferings that were endured by Him who bore the burden that sinners should have borne. They do not see the blended holiness and compassion of the Godhead, in that He passed by the transgressions of His creatures, yet could not pass them by without an expiation. It is a mystery to them, how a man should pass to the state of godliness from a state of nature - but had they only a believing view of God manifest in the flesh, this would resolve for them the whole mystery of godliness. As it is, they

THE EXPULSIVE POWER OF A NEW AFFECTION

cannot get quit of their old affections, because they are out of sight from all those truths which have influence to raise a new one. They are like the children of Israel in the land of Egypt, when required to make bricks without straw - they cannot love God, while they want the only food which can ailment this affection in a sinner's bosom - and however great their errors may be both in resisting the demands of the Gospel as impracticable, and in rejecting the doctrines of the Gospel as inadmissible, yet there is not a spiritual man (and it is the prerogative of him who is spiritual to judge all men) who will not perceive that there is a, consistency in these errors.

But if there be a consistency in the errors, in like manner is there a consistency in the truths which are opposite to them. The man who believes in the peculiar doctrines, will readily bow to the peculiar demands of Christianity. When he is told to love God supremely, this may startle another; but it will not startle him to whom God has been revealed in peace, and in pardon, and in all the freeness of an offered reconciliation. When told to shut out the world from his heart, this may be impossible with him who has nothing to replace it - but not impossible with him, who has found in God a sure and a satisfying portion. When told to withdraw his affections from the things that are beneath, this were laying an order of self extinetic* upon the man, who knows not another quarter in the whole sphere of his contemplation, to which he could transfer them - but it were not grievous to him whose view has been opened up to the loveliness and glory of the things that are above, and can there find for every feeling of his soul, a most ample and delighted occupation. When told to look not to the things that are seen and temporal, this were blotting out the light of all that is visible from the prospect of him in whose eye there is a wall of partition between guilty nature and the joys of eternity - but he who believes that Christ hath broken down this wall, finds a gathering radiance upon his soul, as he looks onwards in faith to the things that are unseen and eternal. Tell a man to be holy and how can he compass such a performance, when his alone fellowship with holiness is a fellowship of despair? It is the atonement of the cross reconciling the holiness of the lawgiver with- the safety of the offender, that hath opened the way for a sanctifying influence into the sinner's heart; and he can take a kindred impression from the character of God now brought nigh, and now at peace with him. - Separate the demand from the doctrine; and you have either a system of righteousness that is impracticable, or a barren orthodoxy. Bring the demand and the doctrine together - and the true disciple of Christ is able to do the one, through the other strengthening him. The motive is adequate to the movement; and the bidden obedience of the Gospel is not beyond the measure of his strength, just because the doctrine of the Gospel is not beyond the measure of his acceptance. The shield of faith; and the hope of salvation, and the Word of God, and the girdle of truth - these are the armour that he has put on; and with these the battle is won, and the eminence is reached, and the man stands on the vantage ground of a new field, and a new prospect. The effect is great, but the cause is equal to it - and stupendous as this moral resurrection to the precepts of Christianity undoubtedly is, there is an element of strength enough to give it being and continuance in the principles of Christianity. The object of the Gospel is both to pacify the sinner's conscience, and to purify his heart; and it is of importance to observe, that what mars the one of these objects, mars the other also. The best way of casting out an impure affection is to admit a pure one; and by the love of what is good, to expel the love of what is evil.

Thus it is, that the freer the Gospel, the more sanctifying is the Gospel; and the more it is received as a doctrine of grace, the more will it be felt as a doctrine according to godliness. This is one of the secrets of the Christian life, that the more a man holds of God as a pensioner, the greater is the payment of service that he renders back again. On the tenure of "Do this and live," a spirit of fearfulness is sure to enter; and the jealousies of a legal bargain chase away all confidence from the intercourse between God and man; and the creature striving to be square and even with his Creator, is, in fact, pursuing all the while his own selfishness, instead of God's glory; and with all the conformities which he labours to accomplish, the soul of obedience is not there, the mind is not subject to the law of God, nor indeed under such an economy ever can be. It is only when, as in the Gospel, acceptance is bestowed as a present, without money and without price, that the security which man feels in God is placed beyond the reach of disturbance - or, that he can repose in Him, as one friend reposes in another - or, that any liberal and generous understanding can be established betwixt them - the one party rejoicing over the other to do him good - the other finding that the truest gladness of his heart lies in the impulse of a gratitude, by which it is awakened to the charms of a new moral existence.

Salvation by grace - salvation by free grace - salvation not of works, but according to the mercy of God - salvation on such a footing is not more indispensable to the deliverance of our persons from the hand of justice, than it is to the deliverance of our hearts from the chill and the weight of ungodliness. Retain a single shred or fragment of legality with the Gospel, and we raise a topic of distrust between man and God. We take away from the power of the Gospel to melt and to conciliate. For this purpose, the freer it is, the better it is. That very peculiarity which so many dread as the germ of antinomianism, is, in fact, the germ of a new spirit, and a new inclination against it. Along with the light of a free Gospel, does there enter the love of the Gospel, which, in proportion as we impair the freeness, we are sure to chase away. And never does the sinner find within himself so mighty a moral transformation, as when under the belief that he is saved by grace, he feels constrained thereby to offer his heart a devoted thing, and to deny ungodliness. To do any work in the best manner, we should make use of the fittest tools for it.

And we trust, that what has been said may serve in some degree, for the practical guidance of those who would like to reach the great moral achievement of our text - but feel that the tendencies and desires of Nature are too strong for them. We know of no other way by which to keep the love of the world out of our heart, than to keep in our hearts the love of God - and no other way by which to keep our hearts in the love of God, than building ourselves up on our most holy faith. That denial of the world which is not possible to him that dissents from the Gospel testimony, is possible even as all things are possible, to him that believeth. To try this without faith, is to work without the right tool of the right instrument. But faith worketh by love; and the way of expelling from the heart the love which transgresseth the law, is to admit into its receptacles the love which fulfilleth the law.

Conceive a man to be standing on the margin of this green world; and that, when he looked towards it, he saw abundance smiling upon every field, and all the blessings which earth can afford scattered in profusion throughout every family, and the light of the sun sweetly resting upon all the pleasant habitations, and the joys of human companionship brightening many a happy circle of society - conceive this to be the general character of the scene upon one side of his contemplation; and that on the other, beyond the verge of the godly planet on which he was situated, he could descry nothing but a dark and fathomless unknown. Think you that he would bid a voluntary adieu to all the brightness and all the beauty that were before him upon earth, and commit himself to the frightful solitude away from it? Would he leave its peopled dwelling places, and become a solitary wanderer through the fields of nonentity? If space offered him nothing but a wilderness, would he for it abandon the homebred scenes of life and of cheerfulness that lay so near, and exerted such a power of urgency to detain him? Would not he cling to the regions of sense, and of life, and of society? - and shrinking away from the desolation that was beyond it, would not he be glad to keep his firm footing on the territory of this world, and to take shelter under the silver canopy that was stretched over it? But if, during the time of his contemplation, some happy island of the blest had floated by; and there had burst upon his senses the light of its surpassing glories, and its sounds of sweeter melody; - and he clearly saw, that there, a purer beauty rested upon every field, and a more heartfelt joy spread itself among all the families; and he could discern there, a peace, and a piety, and a benevolence, which put a moral gladness into every bosom, and united the whole society in one rejoicing sympathy with each other, and with the beneficent Father of them all. - Could he further see, that pain and mortality were there unknown; and above all, that signals of welcome were hung out, and an avenue of communication was made for him - perceive you not, that what was before the wilderness, would become the land of invitation; and that now the world would be the wilderness?

What unpeopled space could not do, can be done by space teeming with beatific scenes, and beatific society. And let the existing tendencies of the heart be what they may to the scene that is near and visibly around us, still if another stood revealed to the prospect of man, either through the channel of faith, or through the channel of his senses - then, without violence done to the constitution of his moral nature, may he die unto the present world, and live to the lovelier world that stands in the distance away from it.

ABOUT THIS BOOK

Thomas Chalmers' 19th-century text stands as a beacon of profound insight into the human condition, impacting readers across generations with its timeless exploration of spiritual growth, the allure of worldly attachments, and the transformative power of faith. The enduring importance of this work lies in its ability to resonate with the core of the human experience, offering a path towards enlightenment that remains relevant in contemporary times.

Chalmers meticulously dissects the human tendency to become ensnared by worldly pleasures and possessions, offering a compelling argument for the necessity of replacing these attachments with a greater love—the love of God. His articulation of the heart's perpetual need for occupation, whether with good or bad affections, serves as a poignant reminder of the universal struggle to find purpose and fulfillment.

The book's impact is rooted in Chalmers' adept use of vivid metaphors to illustrate how the grandeur of God, as glimpsed through faith in Christ's redemptive act on the cross, can captivate the heart. The combination of God's holiness and compassion becomes a magnetic force, compelling readers to reconsider their earthly attachments. Chalmers masterfully navigates the intricacies of the human psyche, revealing the profound truth that displacing existing affections requires the introduction of a more powerful force.

One of the enduring aspects of this work is its capacity to bring about moral transformation. Chalmers argues that a genuine encounter with the surpassing glory of God leads to a relinquishment of competing claims on one's love and loyalty. The ensuing godly affections eclipse previous attachments, paving the way for a life marked by devotion and obedience.

The book's continued relevance in contemporary society lies in its challenge to individuals who remain unchanged by the Gospel. Chalmers contends that their lack of transformation stems from a failure to grasp the revelation of God's character in the Gospel message. By addressing this deficiency, the book asserts, a life of unwavering godliness and obedience becomes not just attainable but inevitable. Far from being a prescription for moral laxity, the salvation by free grace and faith that Chalmers advocates becomes the very foundation for the highest human virtue and devotion.

In the modern era, where materialism and secularism often dominate cultural narratives, Chalmers' insights offer a counterpoint that resonates deeply. The book compels readers to reconsider the pursuit of fleeting pleasures and superficial attachments, inviting them to behold and delight in the surpassing glory that God intends for humanity. In an age marked by constant distractions and the relentless pursuit of instant gratification, Chalmers' timeless wisdom serves as a guidepost for those seeking meaning and purpose beyond the ephemeral.

Moreover, the book remains pertinent as a philosophical exploration of the human soul. Its emphasis on the necessity of a profound moral transformation speaks directly to the perennial quest for a more meaningful existence. As readers grapple with questions of purpose, identity, and the nature of true fulfillment, Chalmers' work offers a roadmap for navigating the complexities of the human experience.

Thomas Chalmers' 19th-century text continues to wield influence due to its profound impact on readers' understanding of spiritual growth, the allure of worldly attachments, and the transformative power of faith. Its enduring importance lies in its ability to speak to the timeless human quest for purpose and meaning, offering insights that remain relevant in the contemporary world. As a beacon of wisdom and guidance, this work stands as a testament to the enduring power of timeless truths.

LIFE OF THOMAS CHALMERS

Thomas Chalmers, a Scottish minister and influential thinker of the 19th century, was born on March 17, 1780, in the quaint town of Anstruther in Fife, Scotland. From a young age, his inquisitive mind and deep sense of spirituality set the stage for a life dedicated to exploring the complexities of faith and human nature.

As a lad, Chalmers displayed an early knack for academics, and his love for learning propelled him to the University of St Andrews. There, he studied divinity, immersing himself in the rich tapestry of theological thought. Graduating with flying colors, young Thomas set out on a journey that would shape his destiny.

Ordained as a minister in the Church of Scotland, Chalmers embarked on his pastoral career. His earnest commitment to his calling quickly earned him recognition, and in 1803, he found himself leading the parish of Kilmany. It was in this small village that the seeds of his groundbreaking ideas began to sprout.

Chalmers, ever the keen observer of human nature, became increasingly troubled by the prevalent focus on worldly pursuits over spiritual matters. He saw a disconnect between the teachings of the church and the day-to-day lives of the people. This concern fueled his passion to bridge the gap between theology and the practical aspects of living a meaningful life.

His deep convictions led him to pen influential works, with perhaps the most notable being "The Expulsive Power of a New Affection." Published in 1819, this treatise became a cornerstone of Chalmers' legacy. In simple yet profound terms, he tackled the human tendency to be captivated by earthly pleasures. Chalmers argued that merely warning people about the emptiness of these pursuits wasn't enough; what was required was the introduction of a more powerful affection - the love of God.

Chalmers used vivid metaphors to convey his message, describing the heart as a space always in need of occupation. His eloquent prose painted a picture of God's greatness and glory as a force that could captivate the heart when seen through the lens of faith in Christ's redemptive act. This, he believed, was the key to dislodging existing affections and sparking a profound moral transformation.

The impact of Chalmers' ideas reached far beyond the pulpit. His call for a genuine, heart-level connection with spirituality resonated with people from all walks of life. It wasn't just a theological discourse; it was a guide to living a more fulfilling and purpose-driven existence.

In addition to his theological contributions, Chalmers was a man of action. His compassion for the less fortunate led him to champion social causes, advocating for improved living conditions for the poor. His endeavors in social reform earned him admiration and respect, showcasing a holistic approach to his faith that extended beyond the spiritual realm.

Chalmers' journey wasn't without challenges. He faced opposition within the Church of Scotland due to his outspoken views, but his steadfast commitment to his beliefs remained unshaken. His resilience and unwavering dedication to his convictions underscored the authenticity of his message.

The legacy of Thomas Chalmers endures not only in the pages of theological literature but in the hearts of those touched by his ideas. His autobiography, written in the tapestry of his sermons, writings, and social actions, paints a picture of a man who sought to infuse the world with the transformative power of faith and love. In the annals of Scottish history, Thomas Chalmers stands as a beacon of enlightenment, reminding us that the pursuit of a higher affection can indeed shape the course of an individual and, by extension, society at large.

www.ingramcontent.com/pod-product-compliance
Lightning Source LLC
LaVergne TN
LVHW010419070526
838199LV00064B/5354